The Rhapsody
Of The Ant Woman

Poem
With
Complimentary Drawings

Teuta S. Rizaj

Copyright © 2014 Teuta S. Rizaj

All rights reserved.

Artwork on cover by Teuta. S. Rizaj. All artwork contained within this book is by Teuta S. Rizaj.

ISBN-13: 978-1495979941

ISBN-10: 1495979946

Printed in the United States of America by CreateSpace

Without limiting the rights under the copyright reserved above, no part of this publication may be reproduced, stored in or introduced into a retrieval system, or transmitted in any form or by any means (electronic, mechanical, by photocopying, recording or otherwise) without the prior written permission of the copyright owner and the publisher of the book.

Dedicated to my parents, Nazmije and Skender Rizaj,
light upon light,
who taught me to love and share the light of love.

A WORD ABOUT THE AUTHOR

For many years, Teuta S. Rizaj has been writing poetry but has published thus far only a fraction of her poems and that at the request of her dear friend. Her award-winning poem *Rise* has been praised as "wonderfully expressive…displays a unique perspective and original creativity – judged to be the qualities most found in exceptional poetry". Rizaj has till recent past been a professor of writing at Hawaii Tokai International College. She has also taught writing and literature at many universities in the country and overseas. She has translated and authored books, book reviews, articles, and studies in Kosovo, her country of birth, and in the U.S. As a naturalized American, she lived nearly two decades in New York City. For over a decade, she has been making Honolulu, Hawaii, her dear home, where she is at work on her first novel and short-story book. She enjoys drawing and painting, and the company of the seekers of Truth.

INTRODUCTION

The Rhapsody of the Ant Woman is a collection of selected poems (written from 1993 through 2014) weaved together into one poem, topically divided in ten chapters, which mainly expounds esoteric teachings. Many of its parts look inward to acknowledge the soul's essential affinity with the unimaginable Supreme Being thus propounding the doctrine that the awakened soul, through experience of overwhelming love alone, can progress along a *path*, which can ultimately lead to a station of union with and re-absorption into the absolute reality. Other parts imply a certain expatriation of mind, engrossment with life and spirit of another than oneself. Yet others are considerably mixed with extraneous matter of the world presenting a panorama of contemporary society.

The first-person narrative of the ant woman represents the human soul who awakens from the state of torpor and then takes on a journey of passing beyond the deserts of the self. Some sections are linked together by loving exhortations; some with prefatory commentary and quick character sketches; yet others take on an allegorical tissue with moments of psychological insight, subtle humor, and narrative frame while transforming belief and dream visions into poetry. To complement the poetical imagery, alongside each chapter of the poem, a corresponding art work drawing of mine has been added - depicting the spiritual quest, dream visions, or mundane events, in a symbolical framework. In each drawing the ant appears at a particular meaningful place, thus the reader is invited to search and find the Ant.

ACKNOWLEDGEMENTS

I am very grateful to my former colleagues Lori Domingo and Jeanie Bouthillier who have read the initial drafts of the manuscript and offered many valuable suggestions. I am deeply grateful to my nephew Norik Rizaj for handling my artwork with care and passion. I am also grateful to Mark-Anthony Young, Julianna Kay, and Dr. Richard Podolny for their generous support and encouragement. Above all, I am profoundly thankful to the Beloved Creator Who kept instilling in me the fortitude and determination to bring this work of love into the hands of lovers of poetry - through His faithful instrument Martha Love.

TABLE OF CONTENTS

1 In the Beginning 13

2 In Soul Unveiling 19

3 In Mirror Gazing 31

4 In the Raged Old World 43

5 In Foreign Lands 61

6 In Pain, In Gain 73

7 In Metaphorical Love 85

8 In the Dream Realm 95

9 In Love Sublime 111

10 In Summary 127

THE RHAPSODY
OF THE ANT WOMAN

1 IN THE BEGINNING

I'm an ant woman! Eyes of mercy—don't look at me
differently! Under this arcane ant calyptra* I struggle to be
like he and she; those long before me made of black mud
altered.

Would you then lend me an ear or two, for an hour or perhaps
two? My song often dries, often dies on my grandma's laundry
wire!

She was a gnatling of smokeless fire. She'd admit it herself too.
Lodging in the mouths of the edacious; what else could she do?
She was gecked into the matrimonial hole: half feeding
on half—masticating Whole!

Garb of subservient fear! The fractured bones of stars filled
her boiling kettle as she emptied the ashtrays of her malinger
(Half) Dear.

Her lambent breath muttered bridging hues of diverse fabric
of silk warp and worsted weft—patterns of sacrifice pinched
between the lips of her sewing machine, passed on to my
mother—a great invention to steal the daughter's intention!

Bleached hues of fabric fallen upon the second "s"
of sacrifice of a silenced intend. Their names were scribed
on rice grains stuck accidentally betwixt teeth; crowned above
the roots canalled.

*calyptra — a veil worn by Greek women

My mother's (Half) Dear created *the whole* name for himself—
brilliant light out of the crackling fire on her back. Grand
historical documents, books—primed words rattling bones,
raising mastodons and mastiffs from their graves.

He was hardly there—world trips, archives, conferences.
My mother on the trivet—treadmilling, expecting, tittering.
Between snoring of planes and yawning of trains, he'd be there.
She saw his back. The typing machine saw his face, then
the computer—a great invention to steal the man's attention.

She spoke softly to him in Kannada* like to a kallima*
on a sycamore high leaf: 'Children, money, in-laws, guests…'
Then a nod, a smile with maladroit: 'I'm listening, dear.—
All's well! Need no worry! Dinner ready?'

Lackadaisical law of permanence lawful only to mother Eve:
feed father Adam perked up apple-pies cooked in the oven—
a great invention to steal every woman's attention!

In the sea of origins and destiny, of this or of that,
the refined strife lied—to unearth the one and to discover
the other, or to go beyond reason and find the It in the Mid—
standing above tether-free to recognize both and no side
extreme to admit.

*Kannada — used as a metaphor for an important
 language

*kallima — a butterfly mimicking dead leaves

The returning rain was a Witness of all. With the hat
brimmed with all, I climbed the brick wall of
the neighbor gardens—stupendously they looked just
the same! So I slipped and foundered into poppling torpor.

Decades passed, then a sudden jostle—a toe itch,
a heart twitch… Walls of eardrum split asunder under
the twilit piercing thunder:

Rise! The bed is only for the dead! Your feet are cold,
breath shallow:—Cold and death rattle in shallow breath.
Rise! Read the Book! Read! Save your Self from the self,
and don't leave the jail at night.

Be Aware! Night is cruel without light: wounds, kills,
and leaves you blind. So rise with the sun that brings the light.
Kneel and kiss the Feet that guide—the Lotus Feet that lead
to inner sight.

Breathe the Book! Grow! Take joy in your growth:
From a step to a step, you'll be led to the Step. So grow!
Feel the Love enfold you now and evermore.

2 IN SOUL UNVEILING

While I breathe the Book, I bid then!—Step on me, crush me! Turn me into dust under the feet of humanity. Leave me there foodless, waterless till I cry: I have no identity of my own—I'm just an ant woman drifted by the blinding storm.

Gather my dust, scatter upon the sea as Moses did with the saffron hue idol of Samiri. O I'm but a puny ant woman till I dissolve—disappear into It all. Then Its Sublime Identity, I shall dare call my own!

I've been an ant in the porcelain pot of the bonsai tree for forty years:—Displayed to lifeless gazes of hominum; exposed to cold visible touch—invisible nonexistent!

Breathed with rancid smell of defiled air; fed with worms of disturbed graves; sprinkled with waters of slutty wells; danced with dwarfs of Pluto's world in the manmade garden of pumice rocks.

Post prondial feast stuck in my throat breeding nights without sleep; sleep without dreams in the outbalanced universe of broken branches!

Roots kept blubbering, groping in the darkness of fiercely
nights: Belligerence at hand! 'Looking divine! Will you be
mine?' Mouths kept on gushing. Foreign eyes what could
they see in water reflection I did see?

Playing possum and receive awards in the mundane breath
of muddle! Rusted, squeaking deceptions clogging pores
of inherent joy of being. One eye, two, and yet blind.
Freedom non from narrowness of mind!

So I claimed choice is mine: If men still choose to live with cry,
through the portals of nonexistence, I shall go knocking till
I finally gain my Third Eye.

☙

So I walked fast and walked slow through the paths
of uncertainty:—The footprints that led to sorrow,
I neatly covered with borrowed vanity.

Then in the moonless saturnine sky, when the hearts reach
the narrow throats, void of words, a compass became
a light-giving eye.

First she invited me to her abode where all the seven pillars
meet. As she embarked me on the Captain's ship, 'patience,'
she said, 'all I need!'

'Patience,' she said, 'is the beginning of wisdom—
patience is all you need to build the golden roof with
the silver floor.' 'Patience,' I said, 'is all I have; I dare not
to ask for more!'

☙

I became a warrior in battlefields, in raged lands
and unharnessed seas—wounded by my own blade.
The self-created enemies marched toward me dressed
in the armor of my past misery.

The unhealed deep wounds bled like wild rivers;—
some boomed and erupted like old volcanoes. I leaned
there beneath Siddhartha's tree, bruised to the marrow;
clouds came and went, went and came but the sun unerringly
stayed the same.

The winds blew off the roof-tops and conspired with the earth,
exhuming the clutching seeds of my many past thoughts
and deeds.

Left on my own with no weapons to fight save the wisdom
of observation, I experienced sensation after sensation.
Step by step thus I was drawn into the primordial Presence:
by knowing Adam's legacy, I was knowing my ant's small
destiny.

☙

Since the day I entered this world with my soul in a pendant—
weltering, turning with jingles around my ankles, fate around
my neck—I knew to this world, I belonged not.

My mother (life dowry), my mother is not. My father
(heavenly glory), my father is not. My brothers and sister
(earthly conveniences), what they seem are not.
So are those that come and go (sweet distractions),
the so-called friends, or with those I meet on weekends.

Since the day I came to this world, orphan and forlorn,
empty and alone on the sloping roof-end I felt. I asked:
'With what purpose to this unaccustomed world
I was sent?'

As the cry of the alien hoop grew wilder and louder—
churches, temples hosted my cloisters, caves—in search
of peace; in yearning for silence. So I weaved company
with priests and nuns and contemplated of becoming one!

But I was tossed to schools and got degrees, buried years
of youth in a pyramid of books. The more I learned,
the less I knew—the less I knew how to know my Self!

Before the Well dried up, almost numb and crusty
as if with transorbital lobotomy, I left to find the Source:—
the Source of sources, the Source of ubiquity.

I flew to far ridges of all-men's lands and landed on no-man's
land. But the journey ensued to find the Hidden Treasure:
from a temple to a retreat, from a road to a street.

In leaving after leaving, stumbling and falling,
in Joseph's pit I was finally found, and brought to the Path—
where I kiss the ground.

I responded to the Call, still in my ears my Master's voice
resounds: 'Full surrender brings to the True Source,
my thirsty child! Renounce your Will and stay by my side.'
I've washed the cup to present the cup empty, and left it
at the feet of the Cupbearer's Will.

Waiting is all I've known, waiting is all I know—
in the state of prostration paved with tears: I praise,
I pray, I implore the indulgent Lord for the ultimate gift:
the full cup of Enlightenment!

☙

Once before, I've knocked on the door of my Self
on the stage of custard-pie comedians—the sound of black
silence was all I heard.

Twice before, I've knocked on the door of my Self
in the galilee porch of penitents—the whisper of a quivering
leaf I heard.

Thrice before, I smote upon the door of my Self
in the curtilage of souls enriched—a tiny window of my Self
opened; fragile ladders I ascended, and found myself naked
before the door of sovereign love—curtana coronated.

Come, I was beckoned, *come*! Hear your heart wants to be here.
Hark! Be still for a while! Rest your head on the feathery pillow.
The seat of reason has served you well. Now it's time with it
to part with a grateful farewell.

Come, enter the house, welcome! Your seat of affection
has always been here. Wash your feet from the dust of roads.
Now you'll indeed walk without having to move—just stay
and keep the rose alive.

༄

At the risk of being forward—to the world then I proclaimed:
Though the veins of my heart wax feeble on this razor-edge
of fate that cuts the sea in half, hear still what my heartbeats
have to say:—

I need to be at *the place* where words like dogs are kept in leash;
where thoughts are left in the heavens dumb; where hearts
swell in the song of the sea. Too many windows got open:
I have to close those that typhoons and hurricanes flung
wide open.

I don't need too much air to breathe as long the air is pure
and clean. I don't need too much light to see to wear blue
or to wear green: a life time to know the criterion of right
and wrong—which way to go; which way to stop.

We all have our unique needs: I respect yours, so you respect
mine. When at times I sit and do nothing, don't conspire
for what I aspire!—Stop calling or ringing my bell.

When I do nothing then I do everything.—
And everything is nothing. And nothing asks nothing in return.
So let me stay put in my cell wherein walls do not exist.

☙

There station me in your love (in today's cliché),
and let me not move an inch. Take away all my might
from my limbs, my tongue.

Turn me into deep-rooted olive tree or lynch me on the red
branches of Judas-tree from the strings of my heart,
contusive in all regard.

Take me to Mina, tie me to the altar, and cut my slender
throat—fulfill Abraham's promise on his first-born.

Turn me into sand dunes of Sahara desert or the lofty
Mount Sinai; undug coal or dainty ruby (whatever pleases
Your Holy fancy), but don't leave me without your love.

I'll chop my hair, gash my ear! That's what lovers like Freda
and Vincent do—when the prolonged cry champs against
their hearing, and only the distance of two horizons set in
between answers to their feeling—smothering the intoxicating
voice, O love!

Wipe out the silent distance or mount me through the stair
of my sin—my greatest sin is my afflicted love, so do station
me in Your Love!

☙

In every dewdrop of life; its entrechat leaps high low,
I look for you! In every scent of open rose; vale of no years,
I smell you.

In each trying russet stubble; its entrails eaten away,
I honor you. High hills bulwarks; ambush lurkings, I grind
the perfumed powder—the gift from you!

In every quinche of life; in pageants, entourage,
I look only for you! The more you become the voice
of my recluse—my anguish, the more I long for you.

In my heart I've etched the picture of your supreme beauty,
lest even a second I forget you. I listen to every thunder
romping, lest I hear your voice. I chase each fleeting lightening
to see the face of yours.

In each mirage set in motion, I look for you! I tear every
sentence of its syntax and logic to get to know you. I gobble
every punctuation on the way to hasten my nearness unto you.

I share with winds drumming my each and every breath
to bridge me to you. In my soul I've printed the book of good
deeds to please only you.

In every drop of life, in every dream—never tire, I look
for you! In between breaths, brimming sighs—there, drop
upon drop, I look for you but You find me: the first, the last,
all in between—the subsisting living Love!

☙

Let me not compete for his love, for I have never
been good at it! There is no room for jealousy among
the Lovers of Love.

There's no such thing as too much love! There's no such
scale that measures love! Love can handle any amount
of love!

He's a chalice of honeyed water with two handles:
with one he gives, with the other receives. Always full,
always pure, always sweeter than sweet. O, the cosmic sultan,
I'm your subject under your feet!

☙

Entre nous: for the one with no race, I'll give my bridge of life
to bridge the two realms—to behold just once his countenance,
his luminous face.

For he's the light-giving lamp kindled by the oil of love
from the Palace of Unity; the Light within Light—
who made the rose perspire into the finest attar.

For he's the pupil of the eye of the sacred existence;
the embroidery of the empire of love, and the treasury
of the Source of Mercy.

I've a valid case for the one beyond race to trade my ant's
shape with that of a true human being—just for a sip
from his Well of excellence.

For he's the guide of the way of the conscious return
into the Original Radiance; the purest diamond heart
without a drop of human dark; the subtle fragrance of
the essence of hidden ecstasy, and the galaxy of the suns
and stars of unknown beauty.

Yes, for he's the cause behind the causes of all creation.
His face, his race's—beyond all faces, beyond all races.
His face, his race is Light.

His name's beyond all names. His name's twelve thousand
names of guiding Light—from Mount Sinai to Mount Ararat;
from the blessed Bethlehem to the House of Odin;
from Himalayan to Nevado Huascaran.

Oh, he's the golden seal of love and mercy stamped
on the emerald shoulder of One humanity.

3 IN MIRROR GAZING

Under the sky's overpowering spell, rapturously its realm I was surveying; tails of comets fondling the earth's slim rinds, as the assembly of the chieftain stars its agenda was laying:

Have you seen those who walk around saying: '*I'm smart, I'm…I'm…*' said Saturn to the resting Sun. Wait for the time to hear them saying: '*I'm God! God, I am!*' Let's have a timely conference then!

Have you seen them how they turn away—they give a morsel then go grudging, Mars said puzzling. And have you seen them using all means to cheat the Truth with sleepy dreams?

Last night, I heard the heaping clouds wondering, confessed Mercury, 'what sensible mind would give up the consciousness of paradise for a drink filled with delusion and sacrifice?'

Have you seen them ascribing purity onto themselves, said Venus, while from love in earnest they flee, revolving around the spheres of lust is made their divine decree?

Have you seen them in their backyards, said bewildered Jupiter, pilling bricks of knowledge, while their orchards of wisdom are stripped of their foliage?

And the Psalms of David, Books of Moses, Jesus, Muhammad…, said Saturn, were made easy for them to remember! And Noah's thing of planks and nails, added Mercury, was left behind as a token to reflect.

And the pyramids of folly, claimed Mars, lay empty to walk
through. And Trojans and Romans, and ever greater
civilizations, added Venus, speak from ruins to make them
listen. But do they remember, do they reflect, or hear, or listen?

Shall we another conference schedule again? The day when
heaven will heave with awful heaving is drawing nigh!
Shall we then see how the Smarty-s would catch its fragments
falling, before the Second Trumpet ends the Calling?

❦

In vain does your will-worship soul rebel, my baby brother!
I ask you again and again: How can you ever let your intellect
breed doubt—when there's God within you and
God without?

Is there a land you can tread, not observe His gentle, mighty
footprints; not marvel, not fret? Is there a place you can go,
not see His majestic face and not know:—
He is the place of all places.

He begets not nor He's begotten, for He's the sower and
the sown; the All-knowing, All-able; God hidden and
God known.

You exalt me when you call me primitive (unevolved species
of the ant race)!—Adamant in denial of cell phones and
fretful of those microwaves!

But say, what's there after Truth save falsehood and doubt?
Can we deny empirically, if you will scientifically, the primordial
(*primitive*) Intelligence living within us and without?

If you look for Him! Look closely, my implausible cushat!—
Where the sky melts into the sea, there you'll find Him.
Where the roads are straight and endless, there you'll
find Him.

Where there's no gravity to pull you down, there you'll
find Him. Where plenty makes you poor, there you'll
find Him. Where confound complexity is holy simplicity,
there you'll find Him.

Where you feel rhythm in silence, there you'll find Him.
Where there's no way out but in, there you'll find Him.
Where you can't define Him but you feel Him, there you'll
find Him.

Where my face mirrors your face, and yours my face—
unable even God to set us apart: there He'll have you and me;
and we'll have Him—the Beloved Supreme!

But first, why don't we together tame the monkey mind
that incessantly judges humankind? That travels high and low
on free rides, bringing home jungle tides.

Our home shouldn't be a rented place to all the acts of
the worldly stage—who sing and dance, as they come and go;
grabbing and stealing, when lions roar!

Home is home where water and air to earth and fire love
declare—coloring with peace every room, allowing Sophia's
buds of wisdom to fully bloom.

So who are you then: A friend or a foe, or both blended
in one? My mind, your mind—let's together crush its monkey
might.

☙

O distant happiness, trapped behind the ancient walls
of worrying mind—you fret to cross over: what else
is to discover brewing on the other side!

O sweet happiness you argue well; I hear you say:
What's there to worry, when your each particle software
comes with the stamped allotted share!—

Your sustenance is more in love with you, than you with it:
push it, shove it, kick it away, and see what happens—
how it comes back to you anyway!

Why worry then, where there's no water, still there's light!
Who sustained the old man in the cave who'd tasted
the water of eternal life, and couldn't die?

And how he prayed and prayed and prayed to give break
to his breaking bones—that obstinate death that didn't come!

Knock over the bottle of water that parrots give—
when there's no water, there's life of light to live.

Till the blessed tomb, when the newborn kicks out
of the womb, the one conferred precondition is to cry
only unto You:

The Keeper of my condition; the Owner of the flame that
burns the towers of my pride, descend me unto the basement
of nothingness with no vaults, no corners to hide.

For dying is a lonely journey—dark and treacherous,
till we gradually die. In dying after dying, death becomes
the sole companion—fierce and loving, till we finally Become!

From the cleaver of the daybreak to the cherisher of
the nightcast; from the sacred womb to the silent tomb;
the soul's Cry never ceases—like an ischemic roaring wind,
oath-monger tightening grip.

࿇

But how in the wee hours in your vespers sweet silence
rejoice—when I hear no voice, no troubling noise.

Silence your primal, bridal music of mind and soul—
so desperate to shut off the blazing static of the world,
which dims the light and turns it black as black as
the Middle Eastern oil.

Silence your sacred wholesome food of mind and soul—
that calls me to its eternal trellised gardens beneath which
the wine springs flow.

Silence your radiant darkness, your emptiness in fullness
of the universe—my core's frantic search for pockets
of pure peace, where in silence it can root and Grow.

Impervious or not! Truly human beings are made of haste.
Repetition so has become the mother of knowledge contrived
to serve those made of haste.—

Those whose feet wade on earth between narrow streams;
those who flee unto oblivion of sour dead taste, and *bedizen
themselves with bedizenment of the Time of Ignorance.*

The earth is not a playground, as advertised on the screen,
to engage in playfulness and get dirty, but the classroom for
repeat students who are forgetful and *plus* hasty.

Yet, betting with my ant's gray head, our God is amused
and delighted:—the repeat classes must go on, for enrollments
are still, still High!

☙

Hear you now how they blame me: China, India, Indonesia…
they all blame me…! 'The globe, holed above and holed below,'
they say, 'isn't what's meant to be! Our turn has come,
we want the same.—

While you played, hearts preoccupied in the chronic Big:
Mac's, Sedans…inorganic appetite, our eyes strained under
the dimmed moonlight when the sun changed its course,
rising in the West—only for your sake. Big, big mistake!'

Shall we change the lyrics, rhetoric, I beg, and do our best—
East and West—we are one, seeking one another like
the moon seeks the sun; floating each in one orbit.

Let's not anymore blame each other. Blame is an orphan!
Who likes the blame? Let rest it on the One Who doesn't
complain.

Love alone perhaps is to blame for the climate change!
The irresistible heat of its blazing flames melts the snow
to *wash Itself with Itself*—after long love making, like one hand
of the lover washes the other.

Its irresistible power swells the rivers, like milk in mother's
nursing breasts. Rises up the seas, like passion in father's
groins, and floods the womb of the heart of creation
with its seed of infinite mercy.

With its sweet tongue licks the white shaved ice around
the curves of mountains and hills; strips the bodies of
forests and valleys to cover them with wet plump kisses.

Hosts the menopausal creatures in a new home with green silk
brocaded reclining couches. And among thornless lote-trees
and clustered plantains, creates them new creation
and makes them again virgin.

In the eternal dance of the indestructible ever-living life:
Love kneads and molds its dough—expanding, contracting,
as it revolves in and around its love-making Throne; turning,
returning onto the blazing flames of Its own Merciful
Self-Love.

☙

But if you and I had the power to turn night into day,
but had no love. If you and I had the gift to see through time,
but had no love. If you and I had the power to bring dead
to life, but had no love!

You and I would be like no other but that early morning
garbage truck: with the power to load heavy waste,
and the gift to make squeaky noise, and the power to awake
the sleepy into a sulky day.

☙

Mine shiny straight; yours tresses, billowing, wavy—
red, black, brown, white—all but guests in this sublunary
realm of time: with gates and doors open side by side;
coming and going at our exact calls—some paying tickets,
some paying tolls.

Passing through the wide open doors, some stay longer
destined to grow old (to reverse in creation from strength
to weakness); some whom Heavens love young depart,
but don't we all leave on the cement of the Hollywood Walk
some definite mark?—

That of kindness and generosity, compassion and love:
marks of true humanity in touch with empyreal love.
Or that of severity and hate, cruelty and greed: marks
of bounded souls sojourning in materialistic creed.

The braggart boaster puffin seeks happiness in outer world—
to find to their dismay only disappointment. The modest in
bearing, subdued in voice honeyeater seeks happiness in inner
self—to flit to the eucalypt perch of true accomplishment!

Verily we all do travel in discourse of truth or butt of mockery, in or without, to come to the end of the road: some with suffering carcans; some with bliss garlands—converging all at one tryst whereby only Love abides.

4 IN THE RAGED OLD WORLD

The Balkans. Turn of the century. 'Gog and Magog were
let loose hasting out of every mound and deep ravine'.
It's from the raven I heard the news: You almost exhausted all
your laughter, now on your bony knees with some more
you beg to please Lucifer your Master.

Incomparable in every sophistry, you won the trophy
of the century. Audiences of the Great Powers keep the bargain
of the silence. There are those who can't applaud, feeling weak,
fed not right—dwelling too long under the cloud.

Curtain pulled slowly wide, unravels threads of your tapestry
embroidered with shame of unseen cruelty. Roaring rivers
picture water red, mountains and valleys veiled in black.
Trees bearing infants' skulls—feasting you with their eyes.

Your laughter used for a warrant into powerless eagle's nests
to break—ravishing their ancient Illyrian native roots,
all the laws of nature you violate. The sounds of shovels day
and night are heard—opening graves to bury alive muffled
voices of your undivulged crimes.

To unwelcome corners of the earth, many scared flocks blindly
run—to heal the flood of their nightmares from the primeval
brutalities of boondocks men.

Prowling in the flesh of monstrous greed, every neighbor tolled
becomes your good deed. In booty-play, you grab the bread
from hungry mouths, and feed with it fat animals.

Irresponsible power in the hands of degenerated race—
slaughters strings of innocent lives; enhances sterile taste
for unrestrained vileness, through storm and madness.

Lost soulless souls await dreadful trial, when savage scenes
may finally end, and silence becomes the burial of the dead—
there would be no dial.

Set on blood no monastery can stand! No stolen lands
your boundaries can extend! No happy life built on other's
death—too short is the laughter with afflicted breath.

And the news is to know: In the imprisoned land of eagle
people, gargantuan pain that can bear, *besa* trust still shines
like a morning star above its sickly blazing air.

When curtain touches the floor, and time gains its quiet
distance—pens will faithfully inscribe then: *Ex Post Facto*
(After the Deed is Done)—you enriched history with fetid
penury.

❦

O don't tell me, you didn't know—heard or saw!
What people—where, when? No, they were cut flowers bowing
to death; petal by petal dropping into tombs made of mud,
in the midst of Blace, no-man's land.

Is that what the news said? Or was I busy in my fluffy reality!
I tell you, it happened then; it can happen again—where, when?
Whose roof has the red moon not touched yet?

☙

The sky's lowering! Where should then a new day begin?—
Should I go out, or rather stay in? Be an opossum in a pouch?
Perhaps go to the market, roam through aisles. See what's on
sale, stare at the overpriced! Read the labels—what's stuffed,
what's hollow!

Greet the merchant with rolled up sleeves—stuffed with greed
like a stuffed green pepper. Oblivious of the belly fires,
which consume, and its seven feet wires, which excrete new
foul worlds—polluted, diseased.

In the glitters of silver coins, his cashiers opiate in heaven-filled
treat of reflection and heed (not in greed): See how lofty palm
trees bow their heads! See how the sun and the moon are
subdued to do their selfless work—each running unto
an appointed term.

See how clouds waft then gather then layer in peace,
by measured proportions water to yield forth. And how trees
stretch their arms to let raindrops dance in their palms.

See there's tranquility before the face of the cliff:—
how the two loosed sweet and salty seas with a barrier
in between meet—encroaching not one upon the other.

And see by the overlapping doors as he was leaving, a man as
mountains old—a single silver hair prying into the amber of
his eye as he secretly handed me his smile: 'Use it to buy
the wealth unfailing,' he advised, and to the busy merchant
softly added:

Great wealth, great slavery, my dear lad! Greed has been made
present in the minds of men—training and twisting even
the good minds. Sooner or later greed is fair; fair is greed
to men the Heaven wishes to abase. Ah, what a waste of breath
is to worship wealth!

With its glitters running into hording, the life of the world
to beguile is known. The pens for a final transaction of sweet
sharing better have them today thrown—for *no soul knows
what it will earn tomorrow, and no soul knows in what land it will Die.*

If there's a system under the thinking head the pillow to dissect,
so the thinking head into the pillow could sink.—'I think,
therefore I am' works well for Descartes' day friend, but for
the roscid night 'I think, therefore I am [troubled]'—a spur do
but add.

With thoughts of her in it, my head became a ruffled pillow.
After a sleepless last night; I've issues with you today:—I'm
truculent; I gnash, sweat from my eye to my toe. It pleases
You not I know! Still I can't help. Asking is to know—
issues are delicate.

Aforetime, a baby girl from the grave cried: 'What have I done?
Why? Deserved I to be buried alive?' A piece of flesh, a sack
of bones. A secondhand creation carved from a modified
fresh rib—the household pillory of disgrace.—

Earth back to earth, decreed by the will of men. Men groomed
their beards with the wraith of honor. All in the name of public
face! That was then, times bygone—uncivilized men breathing
backwards annihilation breaths.

Modern times—a girl screams, cries: 'What have I done? Why?
I'm not yet a woman, still a tiny child—arms and legs tied,
the bed denuded, wild! Adult men—systematic thrust onto
the sack of vile. Worst than buried, like a lamb in
a slaughterhouse, I'm chopped alive.'

Men in suit and tie, a bewildered dog, the instructed child—
transgressing all bounds. Civilized men, civilized time—
the camera's eye keeps rolling; the Internet takes on glutting
five million chupacabras around the globe (per day, every day)
on the sufferings of a helpless little child girl.

Indifferent powers; Oprah takes a stand: America! Pay heed,
turn not your cheek! Indifference is the greatest enemy
to our humanity.—

The plea for help has no effect when no one hears.—
Your chupacabra neighbor's problem is your problem,
unless you choose not to care—the coiling horrors aren't
your affair!?

Even in the bedlam of the new era pornocracy, numbers
do not lie: one sole percent rescued after the heard girl's cry.
Lachrymose eyes, questioning souls, wait for the global call
to action.

The knowledge rests with the Knower; still the captive girls
beg to know Why? I, we, want to know Why?

☙

Though my Organic split pea soup was my upstairs neighbor's
heavenly manna, after the blot of final stroke, she had it
as much as a thimble could hold.

Before the final stroke, she had a stroke of cancer. Before
the stroke of cancer, she had a stroke of life, which split her
family bowl into two and three like a dry Inorganic split pea.

Her son and daughter came through her, but not from her.
She gave them her love, but couldn't give them her thoughts.
Their thoughts dwelling in obdurate taverns of venosity among
those twenty-seven years aged bottles of failings—to bedew
the widowed mother's threshold with a drop of a visit.

Yet in her living room, eyeing the prickly bow of the Big Apple, the sunbeams still come in through two windows: one barren, the other shadowed by a thin plant, she sits on the wool-gathering sofa with her hair grey, let loose,—

clothed in a white dress and purple shoes—watching world affairs go on and on, on TV—serving as the remedy to her rheumatic pain, and patiently waits her Social Security check to come!

In her bedroom, the moonbeams still come in through two windows: one half blinded, the other half closed, she lies on the mattress dressed in a polyester nightgown, reading love stories from a paperback book—

serving as prelude to her passion that passed her by, with a grin, a smile, and sleeplessly hopes for a tomorrow's Medicare bowl of soup!

In her bathroom, with no window: water, hot and cold, freely run at her will—washing away memories, stale and old—smoothing out her wrinkles, lines of life, lined as soldiers returned from wars.

And naked with split nails, split hair ends to far ends—peacefully she lets the Living Chariots take her hand from the drudgery upon shadow to light upon light!

In the park, in the heat of a summer day, 'Would you be my daughter?' she asked. 'A daughter like you, I always longed to have!'

In the privileged moment of souls encounter, you already adopted my heart, I said. I'll be your daughter in rain, in snow, in laundry room, hospitals, markets, restaurants…

I'll caress your arms, wet your lips; compose you impromptu songs, chant hymns by your bedside:—'Fear not, sweet soul, the tryst with your Supreme Beloved.' Your last swan gaze sealing your smile. Your last waving pulse, the vibratory light, soaring to melt unto the sixth sense of Light.

The arch of luminous vibrant colors whispers to my Paani Street Lanai, while gently bonding the edge of vanquished Manoa Mount with the crown of haughty Diamond Head, puzzled at the hearts of the insolent!

Pearls of modern hail and ancient wine race down from the pregnant clouds—unbinding the regal fragrance of the drunken kingdom of Honolulu's King Street.

Ohia alii stretches its lacy petal arms to offer alms to George, David, James…palaceless kings of our abhorred dreams, the crown jewels of King Street—perhaps a feast for the eye in the governor's Tantalus luau.

Sheba's scarlet lens between her brows, takes daily pictures of the hands—kind to her proliferating race—just in case, she wins the Noble peace price!

Hibiscus, puakenikeni, and plumeria laughingly display
their private parts, in the gardens of neighborhood,
lipstick-hedged in alter ego rectitude.

The silent Punchbowl Mount on the left, meanwhile,
basks its soft green carpet of brave souls who were not afraid
to die for the docile rays of the afternoon sun.

Lofty date-palms with ranged clusters hymn their heroic
praises, the martyrs' glory; banyan, macadamia, and noni trees
swing tenderly their stalwart medals in the rhythms of
patriotic breeze.

Cardinals strike the notes on power cables—akekeke, ulili,
and kolea chant in choir the sacred ledger lines: 'Blessed
the roofless (our national treasures), locally-made or imported,
dead or alive—*winters are forbidden under the Aloha skies.*'

Eyes of history—Churchill, a big man! Smoked cigars.
Sometimes a cigar is just a cigar (how wise it sounds)!
As sometimes a man is just a man (how bitter/sweet
it sounds)!

He, a little man! And even he has a family! A small boy,
a tall wife! He, a little man, drives a big sedan. Walks in
Charlie Chaplin steps. No, even worse—can't describe!
A matter of course!

Smokes his cigarettes. Drinks his coffee in a neurotic
alternative mode, while standing at the curbside
by his ticky-tacky abode. And even he has a family!

Yes, even he has a family! And I don't. And I don't care.
Nor I want a man like him my life to share, or have him
in my family. But strangely, God does! After all, after all,
I do, too!

The little man—my neighbor! Like Churchill he too a big
man can be—even smoking and sneezing magnificently.
I just must stop looking at him from my seven-story
high balcony!

❧

This precious plastic mother earth—aged, scuffed,
surprisingly still fertile, bears children automated, feral,
and ungleg—afraid to love.

Afraid to love!—odd it may sound to hoopoe, dolphin,
and greyhound! And Lobo, the alpha wolf, who denied his fate
to live without Bianca—his love, his only mate.

At the setting sun and the setting stars, he stared and stared,
and with the new day, he succumbed to death with his
wolf heart—rent in twain.

Those in wings, hoofs, and fins—all creatures below and
above—unafraid they choose love. Look toward the Source:
what do you see? God—your Model! He's not afraid to love
sinful creatures as you and me!

෴

Once we were all One Nation speaking One Language,
so on the golf ball I've read—but few kids in the block
found the movie too boring, so God to please the boring kids,
did the unthinkable and changed the Script.

As we were One like the riftless sky, became two;
three against two, two against one—wrestling like kids
in the house that isn't theirs; rushing to reach the end,
where the beginning is found.

The movie towards the end grew even more confusing:
too many nations speaking too many different languages—
while lost in translations, they found themselves in goring
violence.

The worried kids of the threefold gloom asked now
the Beneficent God for a boon—to rewrite the old simple
script. But to the kids God said: 'I've run out of paper and ink,
and I'm just too tired. So I'm leaving up to you the rewriting
of the Script!'

෴

Some say the dwellers of the deserts can like ostrich run,
but cannot fly; can hide the heads in the sand,
but not the prized feathers.

Some again claim, the dwellers of the rooftops have made
the habit like swallows to catch insects on the wings,
but eagles don't catch mosquitoes.

Yet others maintain the dwellers of the woods have seen
the lack of wolves make the aspen ail and soon die,
but not the sheep on hemlock and fresh moss.

And the dwellers of the cities say we've encroached
into the leopard's world, but now the invisible shadows
into our yards slip away like spies behind enemy lines.

And the beekeepers say their apiaries have been assailed
by the Bayer pestitude, mystifying the queen and her brood;
now the intoxicated fuzzy pollinators have let Gaucho and
Poncho complete their idyllic vibe for almonds, apricots,
cucumbers, apples.

And the children of revolution say, we ought to fight
the commoditizers of our life necessities, who over the public
blue gold are taking control—pumping, bottling, selling it back
for 1,900 times the cost of water from our own tap.

But I simply say everything that eats grass is suffering most
terribly—the unrecorded drought has fragmented even
the elephant family.

But the black crows have incredible memory to remember humane or inhumane faces—sooner than later, they come back to rearrange the nature's furniture upon all judged cases.

And the frontiersmen have seen the phantom of the vulnerable wolverine devouring the Alaskan terrain—her last glacier den in hope to reclaim.

And the dwellers of Asia have seen the breath of new phenomena—the Yellow Sand, dancing like the thirsty moth that wants to drink from the cataract eye of their land.

And the farmers have seen the seed police of introducers of the interest genes out of the species pool, striking fear into farm country—to set up their own transgenics food factory, for higher yields, more diseases, and higher hunger.

But the Jinans want to keep their pastime busy— breeding gladiators among crickets, as the price chirps high like sparks of flame in the cricket fighting game.

In our virtual silence of the tic-tac-toe games, not far off in the Swaziland, the black mamba gives us the kiss of death, and the python crushes new prays as a prelude to a terrible storm.

ॐ

After this, say to the heathen or to the henchman, or
to the kickers of the sun, or to the chasers of hedonism:
Leave the grapes on the vine, and they live; pluck them,
and they quickly rot.

So forsake not harrows and leave hamlets to erect edifice
and set up hammocks—for the bones of silver and flesh
of gold, for they too one day will rot, and the tycoon tombs
may turn red like lobsters when fully cooked.

Surely there's a lot to be passionately angry about in this old
raged world! Incurring anger upon anger is now ever made
easy—anthropoids and anteaters that fire the harvest, grease
and empty the sea, leave only ugliness on the signature
bowl of beauty.

The Bikini Experiment is made to succeed: burst forth the sea
fruit of their sheath; reduce the bathing-dress in parts two;
and set the triangle brandish bristles in athanasy.—

Rage supplies arms—with different step on the one way.
Fair Reason, is there a way out of the one way?

For that spasm of passionate anger, which as molten brass
seethes in our bellies! That huff which squeezes the joy
of heaven into the gelatin capsule of hell—

Passionate rhapsodies become my cure: blue like celestial minds, tawny like the evening primrose moods, and rosy like red, red hide.

As I place myself under the infinite mercy of raindrops of inspiration, the ululate zone inundates in its tide.—

I seek the Invisible, and as a salvation of the damned, the visible beauty appears—all the colors of impetuous anger disappear.

In the heath of ecstasy and ease—beauty unveils Human connection to the perfect order of the Sublime Divine: For anger is a moment, life is forever in favor.

5 IN FOREIGN LANDS

In the Valley of the Ants, in the absence of his hoopoe, the foundling wind of King Solomon chose to be my twin.

But my twin has no place of origin—it speaks the language of each place it visits! At times when it comes presents its names; at times comes and leaves without a trace!

The withering wind is my twin—wondering is in its veins: with no place to stay, with no place to rest, and no place to Die!

Take my right hand now, and we'll walk to the foreign lands— there the candle light burns: looks at the half city, still in dark, groping like a lost strayed dog.

Silence covers a moment with a heavy fleece blanket. Wheels of vehicles roll on the wet streets—life in slow motion infuses with yielding silence.

A cat heralds the sunrise with yowling and shrieks.
In the last fevered breath, the candle light whispers:
Today is not tomorrow—now rise and shine, or remain an eternal ode in the nozzle of the calcified beaker—
O, Izmir!

Is this then the place, I wonder, where the Seven Sleepers
sleep, and the Holy Mother rests? Is this the land where
the Lovers of Love sacred songs sang?

Is this the mount whereupon Noah's ship by His course
and mooring came to rest? Is this the furnace turned into
Rose Garden to keep cool the Servant Abraham?

Is this the goodly lodging where over every lord of knowledge,
there was one more knowing? Is this the soil wherein each rock
and each pebble holds miracles and speaks wonders?

Yes, this is the ancient land, the bed of Turkey,
where the threaded roads met all saints and sages, but yet its
peoples now largesse do forget—O, let not the shaking earth
wedge them to more comprehend!

꙰

Hold my other hand now, and we'll taste more foreign lands—
there familiar trials, the soul still await. The soul must bear
its own burden, but no other's. The burden can't be heavier
beyond its bear, still must bear.

There, I guess, I had to see a side of the Hell, wherein
the Satan does the job unerringly well. *To act his earthly and
loathsome commands, this blue-eyed envy honored with a human shape,*
as our great playwright would niggardly characterize,

in disguise makes her moves: softly spoken, wearing a smile—
employs with abysmal duties her worms and flies.

No grass grows under her foot. Her tongue cuts umbilical
cords of new lives in wombs. Ah, innocent souls who suffer
her sorceries manifold, run away for dear life before her
insidious plague buries them alive—in her underworld
where she snares the spotless sun!

Any work through envy—work of oppressed heart,
is like a slave's chain that wrangles upon a thorny marge.
Who knows envy, knows no love; evil's patron who
teaches harm.

Benefits wither the crops, like chaff make one weak;
who's freed of them, strong is made like the indestructible
neutron from the immortal sun.

Where knowledge is useless without understanding,
the present state is known: In the village of knowledge void
of understanding to think wrongly thoughts of ignorance—
is to wrong as much as the dawn upon the date-stone.

In the absence of understanding, the pursuit of ignorance
present is made. To take care to discriminate has become
a waste, inconsequential curtail.—

Deep in a paper grave, a writing teacher fears not any
blamer's blame. Hear, hear! I've been accused to be
a bad teacher by a bad student—who persists a necklace
out of sand can be made! Need I myself to exculpate?

To noise it abroad, or to keep their conjecture in the hollow
of hand and not offend the beautiful empty shells and their
patron folk from the library of the infamy handiwork!

To stand a degree above in peace when the ungodly plotting
never cease! Or to forgo, again forgo that is near to unity,
transcendent majesty.

☙

Yet I expect not any medals for the work, Lord knows,
done faithfully well. What comes the hardest—when seeing
the future bowing to the subtle air of dummyism.

When work of wisdom is hindered, into fragments lacerated,
every step of the way; it goes unrecognized or is condemned,
needless to say.

No true teacher is wanted in a tetchy whorl school
turned into an empty clay pot that makes loud sounds,
for the light exposes corpses hidden in the axiom cellars,
and gives life to the barren land through the brooks that
run through.

But the seeds in the wheatfields, parched by plausible discourse through guile, have been deeply planted.—If not now, certainly later, the conscious whiff of wisdom shall be granted.

❦

If this isn't a Higher plan then, I'm but a martyr in this lion's den.—Wounded by bullets of poison coated with sugar for refusing to sell my dream for a spearmint chewing gum.

Sick to the marrow, I bleed, I cry: Get me out of here— or thus the ants die. The half is here more than the whole. So get me out, take me away—the house here is in decay.

In this house if you could just see how those cups are washed: with little care or not that much, no water poured out of them, your lips will ever touch.

Arbitrarily, by the Higher command: I went, I saw. I watered the arid land; I planted all the seeds—I almost got hanged!

I fasted, I prayed, I handed all to the Lord—with ebbed Will from my soul's core—I took my ant's hat, and this foreign land, thus I left!

❦

Engraved in hieroglyphs, Akhenaton admits: 'All creepy things,
they sting. Darkness is a *shroud*, and the earth is in stillness,
for he who made them rests in the horizon.' Behold then—
how rejoicing is the King!

Before all creepy things had strayed and browsed therein
by night, sickness brought the cure to both of us to protect us
in our daring.—

The unspoken destiny spoke to us like to the bride and
groom—when East met West in the medical room of caring.

In the whizzing universe under the subdued Ephesus columns,
set by prescription—our souls affirmed the oneness of one
another; thus we became healing balm for our malady,
a weeping shoulder for each other.

As pearls of tears watered roses blooming on our cheeks—
love in our breasts burst into fragrance of all flowers,
and that nightingale's song of liquid notes, which praises
the Beloved in the early morning hours.

You caught me by surprise like the Alpine fluffy avalanche,
dear Shqipe, benevolent wanderer far and wide since childhood
past. Were not your last words: 'Till we meet again in the next
world'?

Yet the broken seat of consciousness finds this Now
propitious time, for love that's love has no expiration date;
still its unstinted flame can't waste in the aged waspish air;
the agent of the seized unspoken, destitute unknown.

One deemed in pursuit of the essence blaze; till a mass
of murkiness came like the cursed unrestrained rain—
to do what best tears do and sever us in Two.—Who knew,
who knew? Certainly not you, not your devout you!

Ask your overseer fisherman who let tangled in the net
the evidence unchecked! His will 'from your blue bay away
to stay'; my sentient obedient name—no more could do;
nothing else was left to say.

Who's to forgive or be forgiven—the zealots of squabble
in reverence of the race of petulance? We were but faint fish
trawled in the net—the brazen sequel had it so; as our separate
spiny journeys in sadness, estrangements were set.

The manifest ailments are the unhealed hidden wounds,
which only Love's sovereign remedy can restore—
let now its power from the repentant crumbles resurrect
our friendship ties, till death which separates not but unites.

Unto everything the nature is given to be guided aright—
the greatest regret is in that what goes amiss to straighten
cannot get.

☙

Now in this scarlet poppy crossland of thousands Illyrian
battlefields: hillsides twisted in eternal mourning—
how can I ever herein soar high?—

When I feel shattered like a dropped chandelier into two
thousand pieces! When hours in this maze turn into days
of despair; nights into un-responded prayers!

Under the worldly weight, my back cracks—a back-bone
compared to the flesh lying in my chest, which bleeds
wrestling in indecisions!

My bags are still packed; the ticket's still to be purchased:
the next train or the next plane? They shouldn't any more
pass by, or else I lose my breath in time.

See, I came out of this womb, yet I'm still foreign to it.
Understanding of the soul's yearnings heavenward is sanctity—
how uncommon in this above-ground tomb!

In tottered wits, forgetting is hard—the demon mallet's
done good beatings into waves of wrath now clinging
to their hearts!

Tell me then, how can I be wise—when my ears herein
hear no sweet sound? Now postwar noise cuddles their souls,
and keeps them "alive"! How can I herein soar high?
How can anyone with a skylark's song in a knot soar high?

༄

Not all brick ovens are the same; in this I'm sourdough bread to self-knowledge—I feel how each flame bakes and burns away consecrated bosh ties: family, kinsman, friends, hypocrites—countless betrayals, hurts and sighs.

Do you remember? To those you give the most are the ones who see to scathe you the worst! Who is your friend when you relinquish All? But the One Friend—Who gives you all!

Claiming my Self at the price of my self—isn't it the ultimate call? For to gain the One Friend, is to lose All!

Still there's a music to this ant song, but the words can't slip through my tongue. Words labor through heart's folly, soul's laughter—good for this world, but needless for Hereafter.

6 IN PAIN, IN GAIN

The higher the sacrifice, the higher the gain.
The ultimate gain is the serious ultimate pain.
His nearness sought comes not for free (nothing's free).
The breath we breathe between our breaths nor is that
any free (nothing's free).

When the pain sprouts across the soul's brow, the price
is the highest—when *dharma* is *kismet* is destiny is life's
summary.

Through the eye of the needle so I gaze at my sprouted pain,
and see how pain's stitching my way to Him—giving voice
to my anguished soul to be patient; the scythe does mow
towards Him.

Pain has its own lavish mind! Now and then it descends
into the mysterious shadows of the grave—stirring the ancient
faults conveniently forgotten, and adding to its ocean more
salty pain.

You see, pain has a lofty love for itself—it wants to keep living:
by bringing private reviews before public judgments,
and by beating to death old dusty rugs.

So I die once, twice, again and again in the stage of dear old
world. But He keeps returning me; breathing love back
to me—perfecting my pain, for the act of dying isn't yet
good enough!

༒

Ah, dear pain! I took you close to my bosom in this plate of dignity—gladdening the beholders, and gave you a name of a friend: a blessed knower and helper in burning bridges of old, which led me to the ruined towers.

In my cell, I fed you with tears. In the world, I clothed you with smiles till you became a habit and took my soul for ransom—gambling it with my body and mind.

Ah, dear pain! How wicked is your game! I let you play far too long—till my Master stepped in to free my soul, which you shaped in your furnace like a Bowling Ball!

༄

Days in this paradise are forged in pain! I trusted friends who care in words alone. But friendship in paradise is only a pathetic lie.—

Withholdings puts their warmth in the darkest cold.—
Second thoughts make liars of all well intended souls.

Whether the pain's arrow pierces or passes by, I reach for strength above; let not master my soul. I calm the bitter waters of pain with sweet waters of prayer, and surrender the pain's intention to the True Friend.

I'm faithful to my Friend like the sun to the moon.
In my solitude I weave no more threads of sorrow, and speak
of it no more. When I cease speaking, the Speaker becomes
my Friend—the only One Truthful and Eloquent!

☙

Though we don't meet eye to eye—Alas! the clash
of titan self-dogs can at times be too high to surmount:
yours to demean, disrespect; mine what you project
not to accept—mine is more to blame!

The accidents of matter, sundry afflictions cultivate
the Big Farma's tilt and make it overgrow, yet you frown,
show displeasure, demurring through pompous pride,
and the effigy of curing power leave superfluous behind.

There's no compulsion in goodness—the direction
of alacrity is distinct from injury. To nurse through stint
followed by omission, injury—think towering Goliath
is near to piety? Or think you different doc David?

How constant is the strife in befooling, but who?
In contentment now, but where's that the false deities
are compelled to—the good we do is for our own accord:
to amend, to serve, to make the truth manifest.

☙

I've pleaded guilty, for my words tried once to stitch
the garment of my devotion for you. But the fabric was
of bright color, and it didn't at all fit you.

Though we take our color from the Artist, and who is
better than the Artist in coloring? Yet one color only
can name you.

Remember! You entered my house like a thief.—
You broke an ancient lock: pillaged, ravaged, even stole
my last gown and left me exposed, unveiled, naked on
the surgeon's table.

You put with care my two feet together—gazed and
marveled at the Artist's perfect work, and realized how
your proud hands were unable to compete with the hands
of the Supreme Artist!

The Creator has not created any illness without creating
also its cure, save old age—not you—Faith (to you scientifically
unexplained) cures in every stage!

O God, he finally saw the Truth! How was I to please my
thief (my groom), and put him at perfect ease? With Your
permission (I presumed by my dreams misinterpreted),
we got "married", but paid a throbbing price for his defensive
medicine over (miss)treated disease.

Your book of healing wisdom plainly says: *You're not a
good doctor till you kill someone!* A sheep, a lamb, an ant…!
What's the difference under your larcenous knife?—

Now or morrow, we all can be the one: maimed,
scarred,...as a good doctor you become!

Privileged indeed! Your ally earth covers your *mercy*
errors as the night covers the day—sigh by sigh;
day by day.

Thus, *the glorified mechanic*, in and out of the garden
of forgiveness I took you a hundred times. Sore in flogged
petulance, tired in curds of regret, finally I let their flanks
fall dead.

We have only that for which we make effort for—
by pleading forgiveness, not by pleading guilt,
from the flurries of cooled ashes, I at last emerged:
The empress of the present, not the puppet of the past.

These hearts woven of flesh, which by impulse contract,
can easily harden—'becoming as rocks, or worse than rocks
for hardness. For indeed there're rocks from out which
rivers gush.

And indeed there're rocks which split asunder so that
through them waters flow. And indeed there're rocks which
fall down for the fear of the Almighty,' and then there's a rock
on Waikiki beach to which I habitually speak:

Endless waves crush upon you, yet you never complain.
I sit on you, day by day—all that weight! Yet you yield under
my weight. I smash and shape you as I will—all that cutting!
Yet you never disapprove.

You never seek glory. Never seek to conquer only moments
to surrender. All that self-surrender! All that shoreless
silence!

So when the moping waves comb the hair of corals and
seaweeds, and crabs sneak out of stubborn solitude, would you
then come and sit with me upon my beach rock of Waikiki!

I'll tell you then—there's a day in early May when the ocean
gets sloppy, unforgiving. When the rain squalls form out of
nowhere, and the big fan spins into a mammoth foot surf
grueling treacherous swells.

And gray ash chuckles from Halema'uma'u crater,
and heavy dose of vog clogs expanding lungs—interrupting
the rhythm of bemused breathing.

And the raiment of pitch blurs the vision, and hearts become
as air rolling on the eyelashes of clouds. Behold, for the canoe
paddlers in Kaiwi Channel— tough is the crossing, wicked,
punishing.

Yet the more they cross, the sweeter they live their lives—
ordaining the souls contentment as toils arise; ever espying
the tail of eternity, as the foam rises and passes away upon
the banks of another spunky Mayday.

ಞ

It's rainy! Birds don't stop singing when it rains. Don't do
laundry now, says lapwing my friend, write a song instead.

Rain, flirting finch says, washes away earthly pain. Each drop,
you see, comes down from the heaven mountains embraced
by an angel of clemency.

Sing along with bulbul passerine—who with birds sings,
evil cannot think. Listen, how the rain symphony strikes
the keys of soul's laughter—record its beauty in an ant's song,
and do your laundry after!

ಞ

On this rainy day, may I narrate unto you a tale of a day linked
on today—my grandma's tale? Nana, birth giver of my father,
never shed tears while peeling onions. Soon her neighbors
found out the living miracle; each time they came to visit
brought her a full basket of onions.

As kind and generous as my grandma Nana was,
not once refused peeling her neighbors' onions—big, small;
basket after basket of albino, rosaceae, jaundice onions.

The two ends of her living days and vigilant nights,
kept gyrating in the zenith of selfless sacrifice.

When my grandma left her dear onion-spawn earth,
with a laurel above the moonlit lake, and shooting stars dipping
into her dimples, her legacy in my mind forever remained.—

Whenever in my little kitchen with burning tears in my eyes,
I pray my Nana from Paradise, as a pillow in my plight,
would stretch her hand to help me peel crusty layers of
my soul, like the layers of her neighbors' onions.

We're on the slave ship, ant sister. Confide in me!—
Your notion of mutiny grows but yellow weeds, in the crevices
of the limestone cliffs, on the vast abysmal sea.

Have my tattered handkerchief. Wipe off your red brow sweat,
and say no more your tombstone would read: 'She paid all her
debt and dropped dead.'

Let's fly the pirate's flag upon the Wall of narrow Street—
where amid greed laws are smothered. Hold your pain or erode
their gain against your shores of bitter orange.

Cicero dared to take a standing jump into your pain when he smelled your lamp of abused honesty to 'Let the welfare of the people be the final law.'

See over there the light that leaks upon the sea of feathered visitors darting across the estuary—their white wings reflecting the glare of sunlight, but see over here how dark the parsimonious two-legged can make the light!

Bring them portents on horizons; convince them all— their devices, their toys aren't magician's tricks, devil's jokes in their make-believe lie-full world, wherein the slave gives birth to her own lord.

But the tide must ebb for the lagoon to open up— ants to beckon; the Tasmanian devils to deny whose bite is worse than their cry.

No thing, small or big, can outstrip its term, nor yet postpone it, or in fraud be safe.—Mind the hangman's rope patching up the brinks of grave.—

Change is the eye of being justly due against that existence that emasculates, and goes on and on the flawless ship to make like wild wreckage a torrent hurls.

Good and evil are extreme food for ordeal; even the honored paid slaves flag not to taste. In the last ordeal as you gasp for air, the hand of honored honesty shall grasp you off that ship of slaves, drowned in deep despair.

If the flow of river had the reverse, not the opposite,
and the lords with the slaves, and the shadow with the sun's
peak heat be equal—could we then say: no house is destroyed
by what it holds; no ship perishes by its own deserts;
no darkness is tantamount to light!

But what of vagrant whims that daze the mind—
if the Truth had served every Lord's cling, the Amazon logging
on the Wall of narrow Street, can we say: all the contents of
the universe had been corrupted with the devil's deeds!

But whose breasts implanted with wisdom that will not fall
for the fallen men can then say: Teach me one thing to live by
in honor of all life, and I'll be your slave for the rest of my life.

But I should say no more now, ant sister. I speak better
when I don't speak. Mine's not the final argument against
the corporatocracy orifice in every travertine terrace of greed,
the atrocious lying speech. And you know what I mean!

7 IN METAPHORICAL LOVE

Through the cracks of the heart's broken door,
long casting shadows of love ephemeral still reach
my inquisitive soul:

How can the very beginning reach the full end,
before stepping on the first step? All known and said
poured out of the jar of metaphorical love!

Does the end become the beginning without a beginning;
of the end without end, when the unveiling of the True Love
becomes the sole intent?

                                                    ☙

After All! The truth I pulled out of you like an aching
decayed tooth, flooded ant's veins with old venom—
rumpling the rhythms of surrendered heart.

You were but a dream in my dream, I realized in the final
scene—disappearing with a chime song in the wind,
chased by a mocking-bird and a hopping hind.

Yes, we collided like two water-spirit tangies in a lonely
Orcadian autumn night—kindling the golden candle light,
dormant for decades deep inside.

You lured Muses to tune their lutes to awaken true love
to bear its fruit. With *bel esprit* souls spoke out—narrating
common past journeys, without doubt.

Truly then I came to understand upon meeting in my dream
a frank friend—your late good father: you had two lives
who asked for care; claiming more, you should not dare!

Rain falls after all to quench the thirst of soil—coming with
storm or just silence! When storm subsides, peace abides;
permitting you to flow into Wholeness.

⁂

Wait for a new moment gall breath; closing that old door
I'm not done yet—still through the other door you creep in,
I think you're ready to face your old sin:

Because you were young in soul yet, and let fancy passion
rule your mind: you misjudged the intentions of the guiding
friend.

You thought my guiding kindness was a wide open door
to candy shops—wherein you could pick at random free
rainbow lollipops.

Yet I willed you mount the stairs of light, but your heart
was sealed with low desires, and you sought no escape
from their burning fires.

Yes, because you were jejune in understanding yet,
and still knew not to distinguish love from lust—
your each fickle temptation got swallowed in the dust.

Because lust is the opposite of love; and opposites do not meet (though opposites can be cured by opposites): lust till then shall be your ailing camp; love shall be my guiding lamp.

≈

How swift of gledge young days to catch, which direction do you now blow? That which is gleaned can't be overlooked: Oh, I was having oriental supper sitting on the floor!—

My acquaintances from the past making me quiet company— talking between bites of Atalanta (the fleet-footed maiden), who raced her comely suitors, mainly Arcadian, but faced the defeat by the shrewd Milanion, who dropped golden apples on the course to delay her.

As from nowhere, your eyes from a distant table, like those of prank Milanion, on my eyes began dropping golden apples on the course to a thin-night journey.

Chance as designed, laughed out, and took us by our hand— to seek the breath of life, the scented herbs in Shalimar gardens of delight.

Time feasted our childish blitheness—shredded clouds and made them pure water shed into the ewers of immortal youths. Gave us repose on dreams of harmony with sweet cherubim's melody—in the odeum of Mozart's *Requiem*.

Then a sudden step on your ancient thorn, let your acrid blood gush out wild like the flood of Arim, augmenting all your inner thunderous storm.

I sought the heaven and found no fount, a cure for your shriveled exulted delusion, transfigured into the ever-growing self torment.

At the crossroads I stumbled on your rose carved of ice, mercilessly resting on your chest. Your hand I pleaded to help me lift it. Too late—strength had left you; you were Dead!

Your fleet of the past drowned your Titanian present.— Pathogenic! Unbearably sad!

~

A Day with God is as a thousand years (of what you reckon). Time's on my side! A century from today, we shall meet again. On the river bank, I'll be calmly sitting, watching old fishermen catching young fishes.

Through seed-bearing winds, I'll recognize your weeping laughter. Air waves will push you closer to see your bolded head. Pity! My gentle hand you refused to be there to caress your thinning hair.

Your restless eyes shall reveal the sterile places you'd been in search for illusive happiness. I'll confess then the truth— encouraged by the passage of time: sleeping under the shade

of the Pleasure Tree, with your eyes misted—hard to see,
you let the true love slip through your tarried yesterdays.

Ripe time indeed to discover: you have grown up well,
but have you really matured? Chariots of Light run fast!
Have you a fast runner become to catch and climb one?

Dear one, in love with Escapism! See, only the bones
of flowers are left for the latecomers!

I had one way to kiss your soul—to kiss your soul,
I kissed your lips. By kissing your lips, I kissed your soul.
The taste of the kiss was the taste of your soul.—

The taste of warmth that heated my soul. The taste of
light that pierced my soul like a flute in forty-four holes—
giving tone to all its lore.

To kiss your soul I kissed your lips—I knew no better,
the presumed akin soul! In the hurling torrent; in chant
of luring, the furtive talons snatched and pilfered my intellect,
body, my bewitched soul—

As my titan spirit whittled and whimpered—turning the last
page in search for Truth amidst the wind-curved sandhills
of reckless youth.

But how you wish, daring bard Kish, to capture the future
not yet lived: to have macrocosm enough, as well as artful time;
by the revered Indian Ganges' side Marvell, Milton—
metaphysics, mystics to reincarnate.

There a hundred years you wish to spend borrowing the poet's
tongue my perfect ears to praise, and another hundred on my
crown to merely gaze; a thousand to adore each arched brow,
but sixty thousand to extol the rest.—

And an age or more to each soul's part, till the last age unveils
my heart. But as your poet does remind: *as lines, so love's oblique,
may well in every corner greet.*—Ours parallel, overly factual as
those of railroad tracks, can run to Venus but cannot meet.

Yet hope of the hopeless can still in Ganges have a holy dip,
or float on lotus leaf like parasol and be as happy as vedic
pilgrims—whom Shakti Shiva's indefinable spell does bless:
that praise love the more, and wish the less.

Pay heed, kind daughter, so mother advised: Though all men
are created equal (or so it is constitutionally known), yet some
are favored above the others (so the ranks are known),
those who serve not themselves but the others.

Lo! man can easily make subservient unto him all that is
in the earth, save his own lust—his Scaramouch sacred rite:
so judicially observed; how in finery dressed.

Show me daughter the man who has mastered his self lust,
and I'll show you someone who can master the Universe!

≈

Time has become our only dilemma, wise H. Mason cautions,
failing lovers! Between the visits of family members and
temples, we have too little time to change.

Yes, we learned how to sing and play the drums well!
We've even acquired the eloquence of words of faith to make it
almost be, but the world we seek is all too obvious.

We don't really die before dying when we proclaim we're
desperate! When we bring into the house of worship our shoes
of loss and grief. When we husk under the table pumpkin and
sunflower seeds.

When we do to His holy shirt all kinds of alterations—
removing its buttons of less appeal and adding pockets to hold
our own desires.

When we assume imagining roles wearing witty disguises
to hide *we* to *our* uncreated selves—facing the idols not just
around us, but worse—the idols of ourselves.

How many times we dismissed with glibness the *pro bono* glendoveers—Whom His Mercy has sent to rescue Us from us, by asking to maintain His pure religion.

The glory of our image for ourselves releases only its stale gleety odor. The dancing we lead by the altar on the vale of Tuwa spells no rhythm of Oneness.

Now we have the chance, failing lovers, to break the tiny gods of ourselves and those around us. And wash ourselves of hidden sin and manifest crime, if we can break, escape, or extend the ending time!

8 IN THE DREAM REALM

This sleepy life is but a mirror of our awakened dreams—
in motley codes, symbols, metaphors! Deciphering,
cracking, interpreting—a task baffling, not at all easy!
Find a master, if you can; a savant of the Unseen, or let your
awakened heart be the interpreting master.

Through the boscage of deep forest trees—in a lucid
vision of a May dream!—I was chosen to spot Your light:
invited closer Your Light to see, I abandoned my false destiny.

Two sources of light: the sun's and Yours, stood next to
each other to give me a choice. With naked eyes, I looked
towards the sun—the sunlight looked dull compared to Yours.

I turned towards Thee with the eyes of certainty, and let
Thy Will become my will. You lifted me up from the heavy
ground—reduced to the lightness of an atom, I heard life's
most hidden sound.

Then I whirled and whirled around the laser-beam Light,
stretching from the seven heavens to the earth's ground.

A butterfly in infant joy; with streak of light like meteor,
so I felt I did become! A witness I called my brother to be,
so he could see and look at me as the light into Its womb
wholly sucked me…

The dreamy mind snapped and I broke free; what proceeded
was too swift to see—as I ascended with the Light,
myself and I ceased to be!

≈

In the cool September breeze, I bore witness to my death
when I crossed the Wall: all in black and mystery,
I surrendered before Its door.

At a sound of thunderous music before my feet left the floor—
white clouds fetched countless scenes from the times gone,
times to be; placed unbrokenly in a circled row.

When the film of temporal life showed the end—allowing to
remember just the beginning: two white doves on a branch
of a tree were unlocking life's love with a golden key.

As my soul cast its shell behind, like in a speedy elevator
up it went—and into the black radiance it (dis)appeared.
There I heard the voice of my heart, it wasn't my time yet
to depart: 'My mother would grieve,' my heart said,
'And so would my father,' it softly did add.

At that very instant, the All-Hearing and Most Merciful One
bid my soul to go back—thus in milliseconds, so it was done!

My chest I felt almost exploded upon the soul's very entrance:
after the tempest, when the waves calmed down, I found
myself in a dark room, lying down.

I called my mother's name in the most loving soft tone—
my mother heard me, soon responded—the door opened
with my mother alone. She asked where I was; she couldn't
see me, making me realize I had no longer an earthly body.

Hovering above her, I asked her how I died! 'You had
a slight fever,' my mother replied. But her facial expression
gave me to understand, she was minimizing the cause of
my death.

Then as my mother wished, we both walked out to view
the sky's tent embroidered with huge stars, beyond count.

As my mother feasted at the sky's full splendor, her heart finally
exclaimed: 'Oh, how I always wanted to be under such sky—
just you and me!'

Custom tailored chance quenched her long-cherished longing,
and filled her heart with profound glee—being alone in each
other's company.

Where I was then, I turned around to see—Lo! a vast dome-
like glass house I did behold.

Peaceful light lit the empty wide road as we walked slowly
side by side, then I felt my mother was feeling a bit cold.

She was wearing a long sleeveless gown—afraid she'd get
feverishly sick and face the sweet demise, as I did—
'Let's go back, mother,' so I advised!

Having providence in sight, millennium in mind—my mother's
fair shoulders with my childhood blanket to cover like in vernal
yesteryears my fair shoulders her tender hands used to cover.

☙

Days are merciful—cover me with dress. Nights are cruel—
expose my thin skin with a thief's caress.

Naked to the bones, my bones become brittle:
gazes lurk to take with a breeder's appetite as my bare
breasts ache, sorely, sorely ache.

Kisses leave traces of a rancid taste, like the decayed
warp and woof in the spider's net—I scrub them in chagrin,
in earnest, earnest haste.

Turning away from human temptations, I cry out:
Cover me, cover me; save me, my Lord, save me
from further humiliations!

My eyes burst open, still in teeter—like the beam of
a flashlight from the dream realm I get shut out,
in a last, last cry out!

☙

In the depths of complacent joy, I was humbly kneeling—
my palms up and open, facing toward the Source of Being:
praising my Lord, His Majesty for all His boundless goodness.

In the state of grateful praise, I came to stay and be—
thus I revealed to my eldest brother, who was sitting on
the dream bench, right next to me.

'It's all due to my master,' onto my brother I wordlessly
conveyed, 'when his *Heart of the Glorious Essence*, I came to read
with love, the path of total submission then I truly embraced.'

A fountain of pure water of colors blue-green raised high
in front of me, creating the shape of a large crystal ball
of the beauty unseen.—

In the water's womb flowers bloomed, as the water stood
above the ground, yet on the ground without touching
the ground.

While supernal peace filled the timeless air, from the realm
of Hereafter my gentle master appeared—carrying me on his
tender shoulders: 'Like a continent, too heavy I ought to be,'
in my gut so I feared.

Then my eyes of his bare legs caught sight, headed up
a pristine hill of immense height. My master was wearing
a Universal kilt—rendering him elegant in simplicity,
the quintessence of a heavenly prince.

Like nothing I've ever known, a ready tongue in my head
found resting dull; surged like a stormy sea to outflow my
fevered brow—plunging my true master into the current
of endearment ever since.

※

I set on the Beloved's lap, in this holy December dream:—
To encompass Him in well sight-given, impossible!
In no infinite creation containable! Yet by feeling Him,
I could perceive Him, contain Him in the inmost folds
of my heart!

I dandled on the Beloved's knee like a little, timid,
yet brave child, so I dared for the essential desire to ask:
'When He had in mind to mold me into His ever bride?'

A passport cobalt blue He placed into my tiny hands.
Under His Vigilant Eyes, assured me the safety of the journey
to the far off lands—lands of eagles devoured by wolfs—
then to a guarded gate He saw me off gently.

'Do your prescribed duty now,' He said, 'and upon the slender
bridge of mortality, shed off all your earthy beauty. When no
one looks at you; in the ageing darkness, no one wants you:
you shall then be a flash of My eternal Bride!'

※

In the awakened dream of reality, with the eyes of my soul
a vast vision of my city I saw, like on a frameless movie screen,
limpid as a tear drop it stood, infused in airy blue—
solemn and loving, verily inviting.

How my demure heart then of my soul took command—
faster and faster to get to my childhood home: over the slope,
over the hill, between the high risers, and through the doors—
closer and closer, I got to my home.

As from nowhere, by my right side, my guide appeared.
As we climbed the stairs of the neighboring front garden—
a maiden by the door he met, who swiftly a gift to him
imparted.

That was my sister, he said, passed away and gone to Heaven.
Hence, I realized I too was dead! The news of my death,
as having no substance of the news, placid and unruffled
in me remained!

Thus, the journey contently ensued, with my guide still
by my side who spoke with a tongue echoing countless
languages. 'Who are you?' I curiously asked. 'I'm your
compatriot!' he firmly replied!

Arriving at a straight broad road, there a man in peace
and patience at its side stood. I left the kind guide,
came closer to him. Lo! my childhood mate I recognized.—
My very first love; innocent and pure like mother's milk:
kept secret, unspoken, secluded like in a cloister.

He looked very old. His long beard was gray. But his face
was young, his body tall and vigorous as when I met him
the very first day. We plunged into embrace; kissed as mature
true lovers do:—two bodies as one, I felt how unlocked
love bloomed.

We started to dance, and from an above loudspeaker
of an ancient design—"Silent Night, Holy Night",
Christmas carol's tunes soon softly joined in, jovial and
sweet—the Singer's voice declaring: La ilaha illa Llah—
God is One. Lover and Beloved: two is One—
inseparable union of Love Sublime.

☙

A dream like evanescent dew can last a minute adding one,
though to the dreamer may seem hours—a spry snitch at
the shadow's edge of Dominica Island sunset bay was brief
as an expiring breath, but eternal in its protoplasmic substance:

All began with three seemingly cradles with babies in!
With condor anointed hands, I rushed to pick up the far right
baby.—If you could just see: he looked tiny as a pea,
just sprouted forth of his mother's belly.

With fragile care as I held him upright—a sudden saturation
of the ripening earth began, long and profusely as if he'd been
suckling from a heap of wet-nursing clouds, for months and
months.

A young fellow offered me to buy a watch—showing me
some new types; praising them highly for the laced style
and innovation.—

I thanked him by saying; I had so many—showing him
one wearing of Swiss design— faithful to the pace of
time since my college graduation.

Pounding the greening verdency, there came Pamela,
my college friend.—In the subject of dreams, I got her
engaged by saying 'the memory has only the dream context
as a device to retain the experience!'—Nabbing by
intellectualizing the lotus ponds of the absolute existence.

Pacing toward a vague direction, Pamela got ahead of me,
while I got into perusing a spiritual body, kind of apparition.

That very instant, my whole being was lifted up—rising
like a primal mountain, my friend's name I called but she
couldn't hear me—the realm of spirits I was now in
was like a nebulous screen between us.

In a speed of light advancing along the spirit's way,
the grandeur of the sapphire sky by swatting time was
reached—flying through the pearly gates, to behold first were
lovely cherubim huddled in a circle, oh, pleasing the sight—
a picture perfect, exemplified!

I felt I was being held around my waist by a celestial being,
and from the right corner of my eye, squintly I espied what
looked like a portion of a wing, white and fluttering.

I realized I was being taken into a journey to the Great I Am,
while through each thread of breath, I increasingly kept
invoking the sum whole of God's names and Hu,
the Magnificent One—spontaneously resonating the cosmic
glorifying bel canto, the ever ongoing.

I saw next prototype faces of human beings of all races,
like cherubim congruently chained as if by an eternal vow in
a precious cameo—executed in colorful relief and carved with
love design—adorning the cosmos voluptuous bosom. A swift
impalpable light behind them was beaming through them.

Still with nectar of adoration on my very lips, to the dynasties
of stars and planets now I arrived—as many in number as
bubbles under the sea, minueting in diamond ball gowns
and tiaras of tantalizing beauty.

Though all ornamental creations knew how to be flirtatious,
I dismissed their bewitching brow to bring my heart Whole
to Him—for had I my heart's eye on any of His celestial jewels;
I knew I could never have the Supreme Jeweler.

As I journeyed through still in hurling speed,
inhaling the heavenly myrrh of neither desire nor fear;
anticipating the delicious mysteries of the realms to come,
but apprehensive at the speed—which I wanted to be slowed
down.

I started so intoning the Beloved's name only, instead of Hu—
the Breath, for I felt that luminous substance of the life force
of the One, speeded up my journey:—fueled the speed,
added speed to speed.

But suddenly, a formidable feeling of Fear of being taken
to His Sovereignty with no turn or return, sneakily whispered
unto me.

As other most beautiful divine names and affirmations,
I intended to invoke, I was cut short, for as the ascent was in
the speed of light so was the descent—swoop to the nadir.

The return to what seemed the locus of my dwelling
was merciful in deed—my body still all in one piece,
despite the sole of my soul that slithered like a snake upon
my grief—unutterable grief.

Not the desire, ah, wellaway! the Fear, that slobbered
from the mouths of unseen clouds slit my journey,
the ascension to Heaven, and severed the dating with my Lord,
the eternally Besought.

I questioned a second chance as to redeem my Loss,
and appease my heart—like the notorious Big Bang,
about to explode!

For a moment I got tempted to share with my big brother
my mystical journey, but something within me secretly
stopped me.

There behind the scene was a man I knew, whose busy
hands an exquisite structure in the meantime had built,
making me realize how ever easier is to dig the earth
and build upon mundane men toys, than the spiritual spiral
stairway to His Majestic Throne.

As the time changed hands—throwing me into another space,
I found myself facing a wall or what seemed a chest,
while chanting with abysmal longing the Beloved's name.

At that very moment, as a toothsome antidote to counteract
the chocking of my heart, as a prey from my back I was again
snatched, so the journey in hush now ensued.

Soaring like an eagle to an immense height, with wings spread
out in full flight, I surveyed from above a vast blue sea—
shores full of myriad sailing vessels; richly embellished and
in motley hues, gilded prows and amber oars, spreading hulls
with the crew of men—regal in apparel and grand, grand
turbans.

The landscape from a moment resembled the sultans land,
but soon like liquid got transmuted into that of the Far East,
dragon enchanted land.

Now I perceived around my waist a being's hand, soft and
noble—holding me tenderly by my right index finger only,
as he was carrying me in this new journey.

Approaching a cemetery, now lowering the height,
while passing through it, a feeling of unease of the cold
bleached gravestone sight flooded me suddenly—though I tried
to shake it off as being all right!

A new scene then appeared of two covered women
looking like nuns—of modest gaze, pearly eyes like hidden
ostrich eggs, and a few guileless boys, old enough alongside
of them to walk and wisely talk.

Close to them soon I was smoothly landed; there their
conversation I could hear: one of the nuns speaking in
an unknown language; the other interpreting into the tongue
of my mother, the tongue of Mother Theresa—
the transparent Albanian.

The nun with the unknown tongue, using gestures,
something as in pleonasm she said that I could right away
understand:

The meek boy from the cradle, to grow into a true human
being, beyond nursing in a tambourine cradle adorned with
ornaments of the dazzling planets, needs true love from
a True Human Being.

ೞ

As if walking in right where you belong, dreams so real,
so seductive—hurts to turn, to look away the anterior chest
of the imperishable gain—

Like that of the butterfly on Tagore's shoulder that 'counts not
months but moments, and has time enough' to reveal in the
cocoon of eternity the most secret Self.

9 IN LOVE SUBLIME

Though I marched on for ages, and in tarried gamut
years found only fatigue—didn't I cry of old: I shall not
give up till I reach the point where the three Rivers meet.

I'll not gainsay you; you'll find me patient.—
Nor make the short road forever long, but I'll follow
a Way Between—through the meandering tracts, vineyards,
and ploughed lands.

Though I'm changeable, ever swirling, ever bubbling
like the earth, the firmament, the fiery elements—I'm steady,
ever constant in this Your burning consuming tavern.

This royal tavern of inebriation has no color, no form,
but has a high raised divan—a perfect platform for a leap
into obliteration, into the Unknown, by the still more
magnificent Unknown.

Come closer! Can you hear? Can you see?—Hosanna is
Halleluiah is Alhamdulillah is One the same praising song
of the wistful waterfalls; the nature's cunning plot that dumb
the reasoning, steal the hearing!

There're no carnelian lips here to risk unmitigated blame;
no agate brow in pincers of superstitious shame—
only the crystalline self-hood leaping like lightning
in hypnotic charm—the ultramarine splendor,
God's ineffable love.

Ah, this adamantine love—the cathartic that fortifies
the membrane of the atoms of life, ignites the timeless beauty
of such rivulets; the refulgent brilliance of such plains
that stretch to heaven in our veins.

In this great love even to have wished is enough!
So subtle, such a fuel—incinerates everything in its turf:
traditions, religions, indoctrinations, visions. No man, no eagle,
no ant can ever see its beginning, its middle, or its end.

⁂

Tell me then—how can I share this Your love with the rest
of Your sublime creation, when they are so hungry for it,
and yet they refuse it?

How can I make them see, what I see across the earthly ecstasy,
where there is just You and me bathed in the sea of love
and mercy?

I shall but try and try and try…from beyond the sea of all
feasible hypotheses—

But the Voice nearer than near lovingly says:
Those that are hoodwinked now and refuse to see, and make
denial their livelihood and commodity—pity them and
let them be!

From the chaos has to rise up full harmony to give
them sight to the Absolute Reality—thus slowly
but certainly, at the parting of the mountain ways,
they shall all turn back to Me sublimated in the embrace
of True Humanity!

᧞

And when the world is full of men, empty of lovers,
let us return to our sheep where the shepherds get their feed,
and the borrowed flame from the sap of amaranths and
amaryllises and meadow-sweets.

You'll see, how gracious the Spreader is there,
Who feeds and is not fed, but lays out the table spread,
for the readers of broken hearts, among flocks and water-
springs, with pellucid manna, fruit and bread.

If you count there my bites, you'd peevishly complain:
I've sharpened my teeth and eat too much! Yet slim or
pejoratively thin, I true remain—no fat sticks to the unfair
bone.

To unravel the mystery along this penchant shore,
or learn the cerebral reason of this conspiracy, resultant
treason—weary not yourself to grow rich, but cease from your
own granary of understanding.

In the wildest wealth of the Unseen—the verdant scale
so heavy, inscribed in the fine parchment unrolled:
you'll find the barefoot beggar and the bleached outcast
to their due cryptic share are called.

Under the silver dome exalted, thronged around the throne—
empty of banners, drums and glory—love gives birth to love,
and more afflicted love; now only Love can explain
the Lovers' story.

☙

In the menu of my heart, there's always one Main Course—
served breakfast, lunch, dinner and in the wee tourmaline
hours.

Wondering about the recipe!—where I got it from?
No, not a fluke! From the kitchen of the Master Chef—
known only to the desperate few—seen floating like a flotsam
from a sunken ship.

As the serious case goes: susceptible, allergic to all other
foods—my heart was starving, near death! The Master Chef
took pity, responded to my call; invited me to the meadow
of His generous Kitchen, and spoon-fed me with His Love,
His infinite Specialty.

The taste of His Love rounded the corners of my starving
heart:—filled the cracks caused by the sister-scurvy—
Vitamin L lack, and unclogged the arteries, which almost led
to a heart attack.

What's more—stabilized the 60,000 mile-long blood
vessel walls to keep them safe from the world's waste deposits,
and addicted my heart's 100,000 times daily beatings
to beat only for Love.

If this recipe appeals to your heart diet and want to adopt
this marvelous menu, call His number in wee hours,
(advertised only in the *Zagat Magazine of Vitamin L Lovers);*
He will invite you too, have certainty—to spoon-feed you
with the heavenly kickshaws, His Specialty.

So feverishly you gamble for money, my frolic friend!
Why don't you gamble the same way for Love?

In the race you're so fond of—why don't you bet
your world attachments on the *Horse of Love?*
The Horse's lucky magic number is 786—it begins
in the name of Love, and races till it wins!

You asked me to be silly; take the ant's life not too seriously!—
Lo! your request was so quickly granted! Hafiz is now
speaking through the middle centuries, he says to you: 'Suzie,
Thank You! You found me the silliest disciple (un)known
to exist in the Closing century.

She is not just silly! She is crazy; heavenly plump crazy!—
She steals my water jug, my bread and salt. Then she kisses
a hundred times my hairy belly and hands. She sneaks between
my bed sheets to make love to her; in the morning she wears
my Only shirt and pants.'

Suzie, you asked me to be silly! But Hafiz is asking you:
'What should I do with her now? Should I cross the centuries,
and ah! again marry?'

※

You know the way I can get in Hafiz's beehive—
you've witnessed my love in action! When my heart's full of
love and kindness, his barrel of honey tied to my heart,
oozes all that sweetness that can sweeten even the seven
salty oceans.

I know the way you can get in Rumi's athanor—
I've witnessed your love in action! Through his alchemy love,
rusty iron turns into lustrous gold; yellow weeds turn into
blooming violets; midnight stars turn into midday suns.

We know the way we can get in the Master's workshop—
we've witnessed our love in action! When all His Love expands
in our bosoms, makes the whole universe look a trinket Speck!

☙

Before the night stretches out its paws on the threshold
of the dawn, let me ask you now and you may agree with me
later, as you set aside your shaggy shoes for the dignified
leisure of the noon:

What happens when you find out—the shoes of the world
were never meant to fit you? Calluses, bunions, and hammer
toes: your casual deformities begin to cajole, then scream
and complain; in infirmity and torpor have to leave you.

The grizzly bear heavy feet, once you knew as yours—
into those of unspoiled Adam now are gradually transformed.
With closets emptied of Lauren, Prada, Nike styles—
walking barefoot becomes dancing without a foot.

What happens after you've danced with a thousand stars
in glass ballrooms of each galaxy and constellation,
yet the sole of your spirit still remains restless like beaten
with stinging nettles?—Settling with the purposeful forelock
of the kingly Sun, becomes the binding promise.

What happens when you learn after all, life is meant only
for the undaunted? Your head once subdued to the turnings
with the winnowing, now quells under the Love's flashing
splendid sword.

༄

And when you're excessively in love with Love,
you quickly grow old in bitterness, austerity, coldness,
and tripping on contentment, generosity, kindness—
becomes your habitual clumsiness.

When you're achingly in love with Love, you can't hide
anymore in nooks and niches of love where the seeker
and the Sought, notoriously patient to stock each other's love,
play hide-and-seek and hooky!—

Love keeps following you like your faithful undetached
shadow, at each footstep, with each practiced breath—
snatching you out of human expiration to divine exultation—

As one small residue of affirmation of life: naked,
unaware of your ancient humiliation—back into equal realm,
which knows no shame and no divisions.

༄

Since the opposite is known only through its opposite:—
After emerging from the fermented furrows of darkness,
the merciful crown of lambertness is ever valued,
ever treasured.

Had the Friend not willed to immunize this bosom with
the serum of light, I could have easily been among the legions
of coursers on perfidious eventide, wondering eternally
in the wilderness of my contumacy, unable to marvel
His ingenuity and savor His mercy.

Had the Owner of Praise not willed to purify me with
a pure thought, I could still been gnawing like a rodent
into remembering my name, but I have grown accustomed
to remembering His Name—in that accustom-ness,
His Name has become my Name.

಄

When it descends from above, that's beyond my control,
that's His mighty love wherein I fall, dissolve, and emerge
from. He shows me His face on His servant's face;
when His servant is gone, His face still remains.

O I ask for no comfort, no attention weighed on the scale
of water and clay that perish in time—like all unappeased
passions are doomed to fail.

It's incumbent upon my created lonely cells to understand
kindred cells, for I am small—in my smallness I subsist,
I persist to justify where you come from.

Above the market of words, I've seen you rising to meet
the eyes of distant children, as the ties around stiff necks
tempt to tie you down to the fame—unwilling to claim.
O it's hard, I knew then, I know now, to live up to your
grandfather's name.

I've spent forty nights in solitude by the burning bush
when the nights were the stillest. But I can't deliberate over
no one's fate—deflect, expel you from your happy state!

So go ahead if you will, turn away from this dance of love,
offered free with no fee, and pay no regard to what more
I have to say. When His servant is gone from the finite frame,
His face, His love still infinite remain.

ಾ

As the Footman hangs the hat of a ripe heart—
what's there left to sing about? What shall I sing then today?
When days braid years with no today! Oh, I got the hint,
I must say!

Lo! if all the days from youth to ripe have been in vain—
captive by the self, the dog that neither sleeps, behaves,
nor obeys.—

Tricks the heart, squishes, from love's tractable way derails—
today a fugitive in poverty of peace whistle blows the real
culprit in heart disease.

Today the heart all it cares about is to pay vows to the seven
paths above; to stain below the dust with love—with each
motion, each turning to fall in homeless love again and again:
with a tree, a sparrow, a woman, a child…

Today the flared up thatch shakes the bones of the gentle end,
as zephyrs shake their precarious spears—smiting and
crumbling the pyre of the heart into the mire of love:
with a man, a cripple, a roach, a blind…

So poor in relation to this absolute bounty, yet I grow rich
in its hue-diverse sweet floral valley, and hills with streaks
white, brown, and red—among them some raven-black,
like on the wine-moistured mystical map.

Ah, too long this grounded living diamond in me has been
concealed; today its burning rays at last fully revealed.
The scent of the lovers' euphoric pose does them precede:
wheresoever the turn—I find as I see, and so must you:
Love is still is the due of Love only.

᭥

What crime would there be in mourning for feeling so dear?—
One who excuses oneself of love accuses but oneself.
When truth begets hatred; remember—life's ephemeral,
love's eternal.

Look at the end, no wrong is done to the one who consents.
Draw back and take a better leap—when your sleepy dog lies
at rest—the Tailor gets busy with your retailored dress.

At the closing of this chapter, I leave to you my living Will
as a consecrated offering:—When the trumpets blow,
and I'm gone; don't let I beg, any tears flow!—

For this jug made of vibratory clay of mud—where's the ever-
living oil poured in it, a warder over it; a fire-catching wick,
a unique gift?

Where's the life when the death comes—dismissed till
an appointed term, or returned to where the oil always was?
Who rails then upon the cold sick earth and wouldn't listen
of the birthgiver matrix of existence?

For those in doubt, then must know; I allow before the sun's
afterglow—a gentle test, a rose-scented touch upon
the worthless spoonful of dust.

Determine then the cause of my death, and say to them:
Ah, she died of Love, and left you all worth she had:
her undying love—lent to her as a goodly loan,
before the day she was born!

10 IN SUMMARY

I caught the round mirror midway (local time) for
a single question: 'O Sun! Why are you hiding your
brilliant face?'

'When faced with the brilliance of peace, I'm darkened,
bowed by shame to show my little round face! That's my,
the same millennial response, O ant woman! Tell that
to the human race!'

Look then, sublime human creation! This is peace:
Sheer presence with no horizon. Majestic essence with
no division. The catalyst for your sweet existence—
when you don't have to be ready for war in order to have
peace.

Behold then! This is the joy of peace, the Viceroys of earth:
Wherein silence is the perfect music of the grateful heart.
Wherein there's no suggestion of the false to suppress
the truth, and the better isn't the enemy of the good.

Wherein every atom of your being dances around the pole
of spheres of beauty, and death of worldly attachments
is Life made Perfect.

Ah! Peace is beckoning you, human friend: Then why
are you hiding behind the cataclysmal doors?—
Why are you still looking East or West—reproving, abasing
your neighbor while exalting your faulty self?

Why are you trying to build on your fellowman's tragedy
your own happiness? And still, still searching your silk pockets,
lest you find no dime for a hungry wretched homeless.

Listen! The language of peace is speaking to you: A child
understands the language of loving peace! Why don't you be
a child again? Children make no deserts and call them peace!

This is sacred peace! Don't you remember, dear?
The life of your spirit: nearer than your cardinal life artery.
The secret of your reality, wrapped in life giving light.—

The reason why sages wander in tears through the valley-ways
of longing, in infinite expansion with no chains of self or will—
plunged into the intimate power of the Ocean of Oneness.

Look! This is supernal peace! Who needs the head resting on
the comfort of the neck, and the boneless tongue that restlessly
talks and talks of peace?

Look, at the prints of singularity in creation made serviceable
onto you like the gardener in your own heart's garden:—
uproot those violent traitor's weeds, and plant instead floral
wonders of eternal Peace.

❧

In summary, I, the ant woman, I still remain one—
crawling, singing under the hot Hawaiian sun about the ways
to reach union with the Beloved One:

Let's start with: Visit your empty grave, and begin writing
your own epitaph. Walk through an ancient city in ruins,
and see where the corrupters and prodigals end. Pay homage
to a saint's tomb, and see how saints do not die,
but they Become!

Do your onerous duty then: Clean all the corners of your
house, and remove all your facial make-up. Climb the Fuji
Mountain, and jump into life on the parachute of Faith.—

Cross the Amazon River, and give all your attachments
to a crocodile. Smell a rose in full bloom, and prick your
heart on its thorns.

Feed a hungry parched mouth. Stroke the hair of an orphan,
and pay his school tuition. Smile to a distressed passer-by,
and buy her a larger size of shoes. Wash the feet of your
parents—then drink the washing water.

Next: Pull the chair under your pride. Kiss the ground
were Prophets walked. Bruise your knees on prayer rug.
Go on pilgrimage and circle the heavens, and deflate your
bloated belly by fasting for a decade.

Cover your head with a dozen blankets. Lick the wounds
of a Molokai leper. Donate your kidney to an Albanian or
a Rwandan refugee, and build a church, a mosque, or a temple
in the center of Las Vegas City.

Cover the others' faults and laugh at yours. Listen to folly
with your ears plugged. Watch lewdness with your eyes closed.
Halt the shower of bats falling on the beds of defeated men.

Learn the language of birds and ants, then teach it to the deaf
and mute. Forgive landlords, presidents, doctors in blood–
stained white uniforms, and plant a tree for your enemy's
posterity.

Moreover: Toss all your books into a donkey's pit,
and pick on your break-outs to get scientifically inspired.
Buy a compass to get to the sun—steal its light and give it
to the blind. And speak not even when given a continent of oil
in a *zoon politikon* rally.

If you get somehow stuck on the way: Find a spiritual Master
specialized in cracking coconut heads. Burn all the bridges
of your old taverns. Purchase garments with no pockets.
Throw a banquet for God's drunkards, gamblers, and clowns,
and do your duty well to please God only.

Spend forty years in a cave. Spend forty other years scrubbing
the world's toilets. Stand on one leg to get your rest.
Receive a wayfarer as an overnight guest, and give him all
your fortune for the rest of his journey.

Join a caravan of the desert Bedouins. Offer your polished
heart as a mirror to a stranger. Share your gifts of divine
treasure even with those who mock and devalue. And color
your ninety-nine billion breaths with remembrance of God.

Finally: Forget all the above:—
For the quickest way to reach union with the Beloved
One—just tear all your clothes and dance naked in
the middle of CEO meeting, and sing the anthem of
Love, Love, Love

ം

Ah, my fellow ant, this my rhapsody in this anthill can
never end.—It brought me to my knees, for I was willing
to bend. Outgrew my bounds; strived not to solve them.—

Here again, with a voice to sing as tiny in puny, I sing
anyway, till the day when the world is empty of men
and full of Lovers!

Made in the USA
Lexington, KY
02 April 2014